Ballet Teacher Lesson Planner

Teacher: _____

School: _____

Year: _____

Year-Long Overview

Level _____ Day/Time _____

MODULE #:	CHOREOGRAPHY & NOTES
Date:	
Objectives:	

MODULE #:	CHOREOGRAPHY & NOTES
Date:	
Objectives:	

Year-Long Overview

Level _____   Day/Time _____

MODULE #:

Date:

Objectives:

CHOREOGRAPHY & NOTES

MODULE #:

Date:

Objectives:

CHOREOGRAPHY & NOTES

Year-Long Overview

Level _____ Day/Time _____

MODULE #:

Date:

Objectives:

CHOREOGRAPHY & NOTES

MODULE #:

Date:

Objectives:

CHOREOGRAPHY & NOTES

Year-Long Overview

Level _____ Day/Time _____

MODULE #:	CHOREOGRAPHY & NOTES
Date:	
Objectives:	

MODULE #:	CHOREOGRAPHY & NOTES
Date:	
Objectives:	

Year-Long Overview

Level _____ Day/Time _____

MODULE #:

Date:

Objectives:

CHOREOGRAPHY & NOTES

MODULE #:

Date:

Objectives:

CHOREOGRAPHY & NOTES

Year-Long Overview

Level _____   Day/Time _____

MODULE #:	CHOREOGRAPHY & NOTES
Date: Objectives:	

MODULE #:	CHOREOGRAPHY & NOTES
Date: Objectives:	

Year-Long Overview

Level _____ Day/Time _____

MODULE #:

Date:

Objectives:

CHOREOGRAPHY & NOTES

MODULE #:

Date:

Objectives:

CHOREOGRAPHY & NOTES

Year-Long Overview

Level _____ Day/Time _____

MODULE #:	CHOREOGRAPHY & NOTES
Date:	
Objectives:	

MODULE #:	CHOREOGRAPHY & NOTES
Date:	
Objectives:	

Lesson Plan

Lesson # _____

| OBJECTIVES | EXERCISES & COMBINATIONS
and variations |
|---|---|
| | |

Lesson Plan

Lesson # _____

MUSIC	NOTES

Lesson Plan

Lesson # _____

OBJECTIVES	EXERCISES & COMBINATIONS and variations

Lesson Plan

Lesson # _____

MUSIC	NOTES

Lesson Plan

Lesson # _____

OBJECTIVES	EXERCISES & COMBINATIONS
	and variations

Lesson Plan

Lesson # _____

MUSIC

NOTES

Lesson Plan

Lesson # _____

OBJECTIVES	EXERCISES & COMBINATIONS and variations

Lesson Plan

Lesson # _____

MUSIC	NOTES

Lesson Plan

Lesson # _____

OBJECTIVES	EXERCISES & COMBINATIONS and variations

Lesson Plan

Lesson # _____

MUSIC	NOTES

Lesson Plan

Lesson # _____

OBJECTIVES	EXERCISES & COMBINATIONS and variations

Lesson Plan

Lesson # _____

MUSIC

NOTES

Lesson Plan

Lesson # _____

OBJECTIVES	EXERCISES & COMBINATIONS and variations

Lesson Plan

Lesson # _____

MUSIC

NOTES

Lesson Plan

Lesson # _____

OBJECTIVES	EXERCISES & COMBINATIONS
	and variations

Lesson Plan

Lesson # _____

MUSIC

NOTES

Lesson Plan

Lesson # _____

OBJECTIVES	EXERCISES & COMBINATIONS and variations

Lesson Plan

Lesson # _____

MUSIC	NOTES

Lesson Plan

Lesson # _____

OBJECTIVES	EXERCISES & COMBINATIONS and variations

Lesson Plan

Lesson # _____

MUSIC

NOTES

Lesson Plan

Lesson # _____

OBJECTIVES	EXERCISES & COMBINATIONS
	and variations

Lesson Plan

Lesson # _____

MUSIC	NOTES

Lesson Plan

Lesson # _____

OBJECTIVES	EXERCISES & COMBINATIONS and variations

Lesson Plan

Lesson # _____

MUSIC

NOTES

Lesson Plan

Lesson # _____

OBJECTIVES	EXERCISES & COMBINATIONS and variations

Lesson Plan

Lesson # _____

MUSIC

NOTES

Lesson Plan

Lesson # _____

OBJECTIVES	EXERCISES & COMBINATIONS
	and variations

Lesson Plan

Lesson # _____

MUSIC	NOTES

Lesson Plan

Lesson # _____

OBJECTIVES	EXERCISES & COMBINATIONS and variations

Lesson Plan

Lesson # _____

MUSIC	NOTES

Lesson Plan

Lesson # _____

OBJECTIVES	EXERCISES & COMBINATIONS
	and variations

Lesson Plan

Lesson # _____

MUSIC

NOTES

Lesson Plan

Lesson # _____

OBJECTIVES	EXERCISES & COMBINATIONS and variations

Lesson Plan

Lesson # _____

MUSIC

NOTES

Lesson Plan

Lesson # _____

OBJECTIVES	EXERCISES & COMBINATIONS
	and variations

Lesson Plan

Lesson # _____

MUSIC	NOTES

Lesson Plan

Lesson # _____

OBJECTIVES	EXERCISES & COMBINATIONS
	and variations

Lesson Plan

Lesson # _____

MUSIC

NOTES

Lesson Plan

Lesson # _____

OBJECTIVES	EXERCISES & COMBINATIONS and variations

Lesson Plan

Lesson # _____

MUSIC

NOTES

Lesson Plan

Lesson # _____

OBJECTIVES	EXERCISES & COMBINATIONS and variations

Lesson Plan

Lesson # _____

MUSIC

NOTES

Lesson Plan

Lesson # _____

OBJECTIVES	EXERCISES & COMBINATIONS and variations

Lesson Plan

Lesson # _____

MUSIC	NOTES

Lesson Plan

Lesson # _____

OBJECTIVES	EXERCISES & COMBINATIONS and variations

Lesson Plan

Lesson # _____

MUSIC

NOTES

Lesson Plan

Lesson # _____

OBJECTIVES	EXERCISES & COMBINATIONS
	and variations

Lesson Plan

Lesson # _____

MUSIC	NOTES

Lesson Plan

Lesson # _____

OBJECTIVES	EXERCISES & COMBINATIONS and variations

Lesson Plan

Lesson # _____

MUSIC

NOTES

Lesson Plan

Lesson # _____

OBJECTIVES	EXERCISES & COMBINATIONS and variations

Lesson Plan

Lesson # _____

MUSIC

NOTES

Lesson Plan

Lesson # _____

OBJECTIVES

EXERCISES & COMBINATIONS
and variations

Lesson Plan

Lesson # _____

MUSIC

NOTES

Lesson Plan

Lesson # _____

OBJECTIVES	EXERCISES & COMBINATIONS
	and variations

Lesson Plan

Lesson # _____

MUSIC

NOTES

Lesson Plan

Lesson # _____

OBJECTIVES	EXERCISES & COMBINATIONS
	and variations

Lesson Plan

Lesson # _____

MUSIC	NOTES

Lesson Plan

Lesson # _____

OBJECTIVES	EXERCISES & COMBINATIONS and variations

Lesson Plan

Lesson # _____

MUSIC

NOTES

Lesson Plan

Lesson # _____

OBJECTIVES	EXERCISES & COMBINATIONS and variations

Lesson Plan

Lesson # _____

MUSIC

NOTES

Lesson Plan

Lesson # _____

OBJECTIVES	EXERCISES & COMBINATIONS and variations

Lesson Plan

Lesson # _____

MUSIC	NOTES

Lesson Plan

Lesson # _____

OBJECTIVES	EXERCISES & COMBINATIONS
	and variations

Lesson Plan

Lesson # _____

MUSIC	NOTES

Lesson Plan

Lesson # _____

OBJECTIVES	EXERCISES & COMBINATIONS
	and variations

Lesson Plan

Lesson # _____

MUSIC

NOTES

Lesson Plan

Lesson # _____

OBJECTIVES	EXERCISES & COMBINATIONS and variations

Lesson Plan

Lesson # _____

MUSIC

NOTES

Lesson Plan

Lesson # _____

OBJECTIVES	EXERCISES & COMBINATIONS and variations

Lesson Plan

Lesson # _____

MUSIC	NOTES

Lesson Plan

Lesson # _____

OBJECTIVES	EXERCISES & COMBINATIONS and variations

Lesson Plan

Lesson # _____

MUSIC

NOTES

Lesson Plan

Lesson # _____

OBJECTIVES	EXERCISES & COMBINATIONS
	and variations

Lesson Plan

Lesson # _____

MUSIC	NOTES

Lesson Plan

Lesson # _____

| OBJECTIVES | EXERCISES & COMBINATIONS
and variations |
|---|---|
| | |

Lesson Plan

Lesson # _____

MUSIC	NOTES

Lesson Plan

Lesson # _____

OBJECTIVES	EXERCISES & COMBINATIONS and variations

Lesson Plan

Lesson # _____

MUSIC

NOTES

Lesson Plan

Lesson # _____

OBJECTIVES	EXERCISES & COMBINATIONS
	and variations

Lesson Plan

Lesson # _____

MUSIC

NOTES

Lesson Plan

Lesson # _____

OBJECTIVES	EXERCISES & COMBINATIONS and variations

Lesson Plan

Lesson # _____

MUSIC	NOTES

Lesson Plan

Lesson # _____

OBJECTIVES	EXERCISES & COMBINATIONS and variations

Lesson Plan

Lesson # _____

MUSIC

NOTES

Lesson Plan

Lesson # _____

OBJECTIVES	EXERCISES & COMBINATIONS
	and variations

Lesson Plan

Lesson # _____

MUSIC	NOTES

Lesson Plan

Lesson # _____

OBJECTIVES	EXERCISES & COMBINATIONS and variations

Lesson Plan

Lesson # _____

MUSIC	NOTES

Lesson Plan

Lesson # _____

OBJECTIVES	EXERCISES & COMBINATIONS and variations

Lesson Plan

Lesson # _____

MUSIC	NOTES

Class Groupings

Level _____ Day/Time _____

GROUP #:

STRENGTHS & WEAKNESSES

GROUP #:

STRENGTHS & WEAKNESSES

Class Groupings

Level _____ Day/Time _____

GROUP #:	STRENGTHS & WEAKNESSES

GROUP #:	STRENGTHS & WEAKNESSES

Class Groupings

Level _____ Day/Time _____

GROUP #:	STRENGTHS & WEAKNESSES

GROUP #:	STRENGTHS & WEAKNESSES

Class Groupings

Level _____ Day/Time _____

GROUP #:	STRENGTHS & WEAKNESSES

GROUP #:	STRENGTHS & WEAKNESSES

Class Groupings

Level _____ Day/Time _____

GROUP #:	STRENGTHS & WEAKNESSES

GROUP #:	STRENGTHS & WEAKNESSES

Class Groupings

Level _____ Day/Time _____

GROUP #:	STRENGTHS & WEAKNESSES

GROUP #:	STRENGTHS & WEAKNESSES

Class Groupings

Level _____ Day/Time _____

GROUP #:

STRENGTHS & WEAKNESSES

GROUP #:

STRENGTHS & WEAKNESSES

Class Groupings

Level _____ Day/Time _____

GROUP #:	STRENGTHS & WEAKNESSES

GROUP #:	STRENGTHS & WEAKNESSES

Combination

Exercise _____ Level _____

APPROPRIATE SONGS

COMBINATION & NOTES

VARIATIONS

Combination

Exercise _____ Level _____

APPROPRIATE SONGS

VARIATIONS

COMBINATION & NOTES

Combination

Exercise _____ Level _____

APPROPRIATE SONGS

COMBINATION & NOTES

VARIATIONS

Combination

Exercise _____ Level _____

APPROPRIATE SONGS

VARIATIONS

COMBINATION & NOTES

Combination

Exercise _____ Level _____

APPROPRIATE SONGS

COMBINATION & NOTES

VARIATIONS

Combination

Exercise _____ Level _____

APPROPRIATE SONGS

VARIATIONS

COMBINATION & NOTES

Combination

Exercise _____ Level _____

APPROPRIATE SONGS

VARIATIONS

COMBINATION & NOTES

Combination

Exercise _____ Level _____

APPROPRIATE SONGS

COMBINATION & NOTES

VARIATIONS

Combination

Exercise _____ Level _____

APPROPRIATE SONGS

COMBINATION & NOTES

VARIATIONS

Combination

Exercise _____ Level _____

APPROPRIATE SONGS

COMBINATION & NOTES

VARIATIONS

Student's Center Spots

Level _____ Day/Time _____

Student's Center Spots

Level _____ Day/Time _____

X   X   X   X   X   X   X

   X   X   X   X   X   X

X   X   X   X   X   X   X

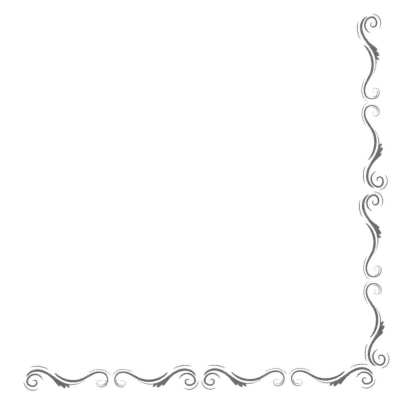

Student's Center Spots

Level _____ Day/Time _____

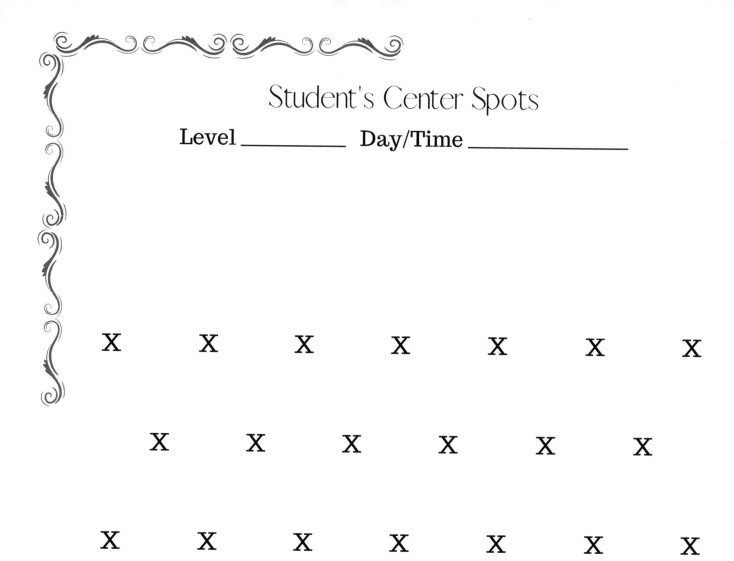

Student's Center Spots

Level _____ Day/Time _____

X   X   X   X   X   X   X

     X   X   X   X   X   X

X   X   X   X   X   X   X

Student's Center Spots

Level _____   Day/Time _____

X   X   X   X   X   X   X

   X   X   X   X   X   X

X   X   X   X   X   X   X

Student's Center Spots

Level _____ Day/Time _____

X   X   X   X   X   X   X

   X   X   X   X   X   X

X   X   X   X   X   X   X

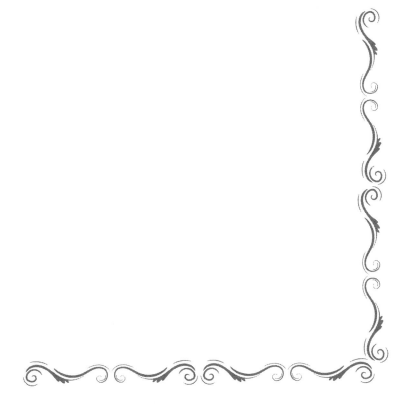

Student's Barre Spots

Level _____ Day/Time _____

Student's Barre Spots

Level _____ Day/Time _____

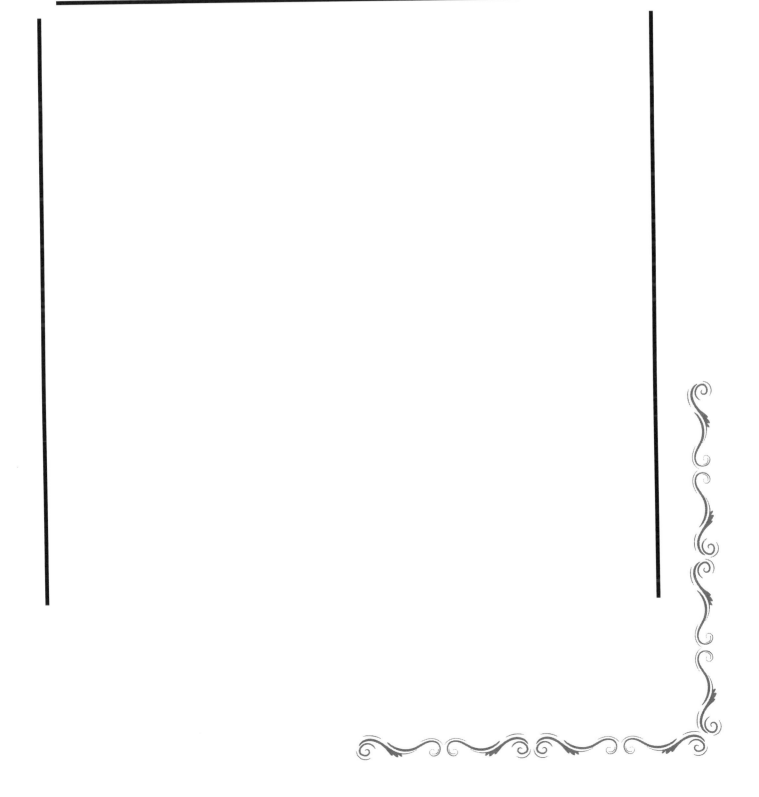

Student's Barre Spots

Level _____ Day/Time _____

Student's Barre Spots

Level _____   Day/Time _____

Student's Barre Spots

Level _____ Day/Time _____

Student's Barre Spots

Level _____   Day/Time _____

Student's Spots

Level _____ Day/Time _____

Student's Spots

Level _____   Day/Time _____

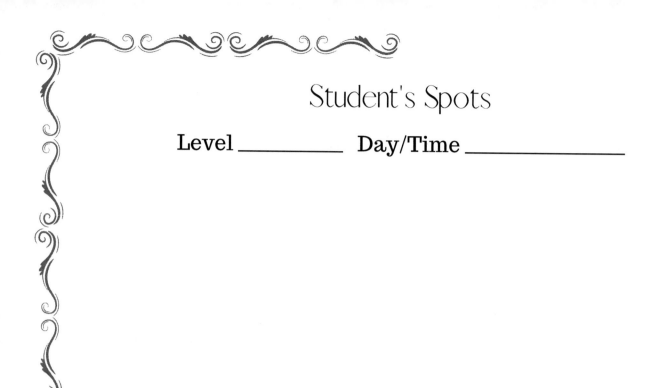

Student's Spots

Level _____ Day/Time _____

Student's Spots

Level _____ Day/Time _____

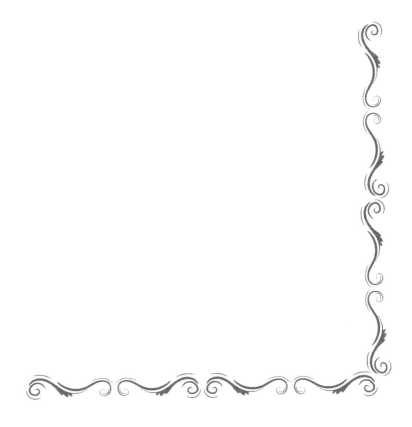

Student's Spots

Level _____ Day/Time _____

Student's Spots

Level _____ Day/Time _____

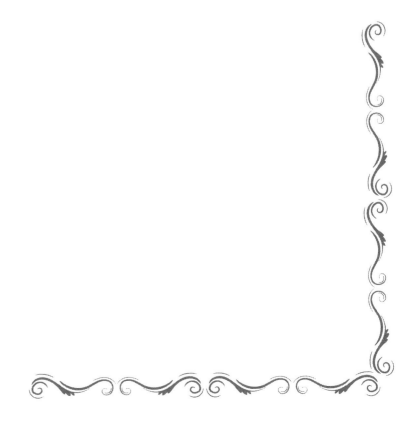

Student Information

Level _____ Day/Time _____

Name	Birthday	Parent Contact #

Student Information

Level _____ Day/Time _____

Name	Birthday	Parent Contact #

Student Information

Level _____ Day/Time _____

Name	Birthday	Parent Contact #

Student Information

Level _____ Day/Time _____

Name	Birthday	Parent Contact #

Student Information

Level _____ Day/Time _____

Name	Birthday	Parent Contact #

Student Information

Level _____ Day/Time _____

Name	Birthday	Parent Contact #

Student Information

Level _____ Day/Time _____

Name	Birthday	Parent Contact #

Student Information

Level _____   Day/Time _____

Name	Birthday	Parent Contact #

Student Info

Level _____   Day/Time _____

Name   Age   Stronger Foot

Strengths, Weaknesses & Notes

Student Info

Level _____ Day/Time _____

Name	Age	Stronger Foot

Strengths, Weaknesses & Notes

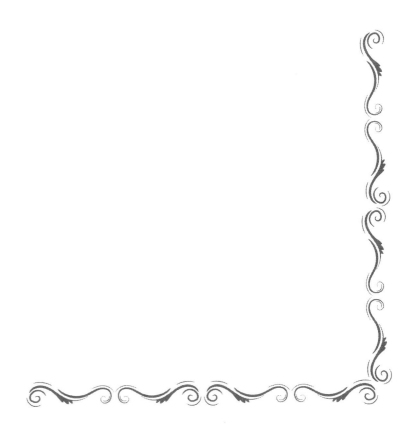

Student Info

Level _____ Day/Time _____

Name   Age   Stronger Foot

Strengths, Weaknesses & Notes

Student Info

Level _____   Day/Time _____

Name	Age	Stronger Foot

Strengths, Weaknesses & Notes

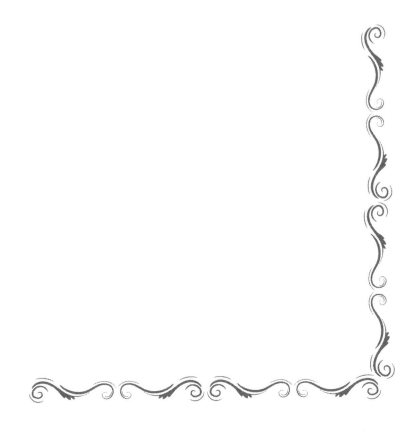

Student Info

Level _____   Day/Time _____

Name   Age   Stronger Foot

Strengths, Weaknesses & Notes

Student Info

Level _____ Day/Time _____

Name	Age	Stronger Foot

Strengths, Weaknesses & Notes

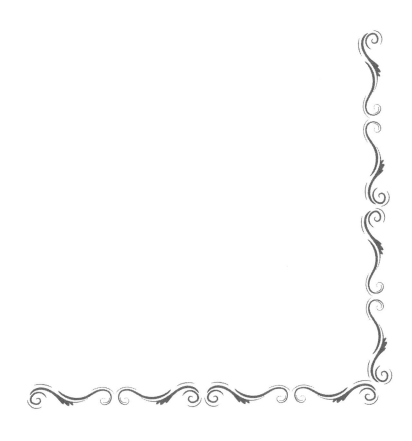

Student Info

Level _____ Day/Time _____

Name   Age   Stronger Foot

Strengths, Weaknesses & Notes

Student Info

Level _____ Day/Time _____

Name	Age	Stronger Foot

Strengths, Weaknesses & Notes

Student Info

Level _____ Day/Time _____

Name	Age	Stronger Foot

Strengths, Weaknesses & Notes

Student Info

Level _____ Day/Time _____

Name	Age	Stronger Foot

Strengths, Weaknesses & Notes

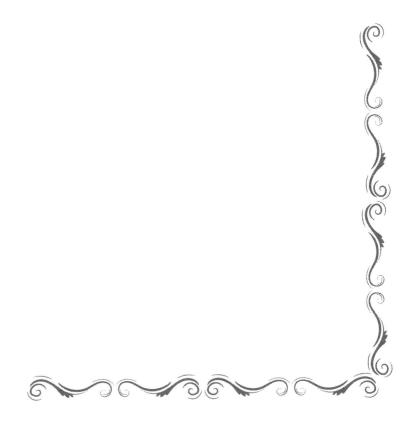

Student Info

Level _____ Day/Time _____

Name	Age	Stronger Foot

Strengths, Weaknesses & Notes

Student Info

Level _____ Day/Time _____

Name	Age	Stronger Foot

Strengths, Weaknesses & Notes

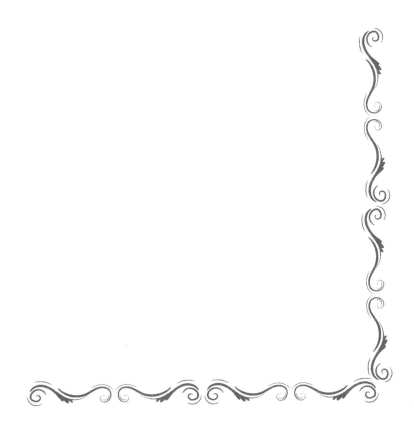

Student Info

Level _____ Day/Time _____

Name   Age   Stronger Foot

Strengths, Weaknesses & Notes

Student Info

Level _____ Day/Time _____

Name	Age	Stronger Foot

Strengths, Weaknesses & Notes

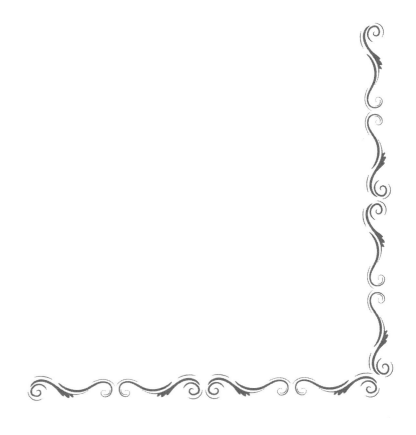

Student Info

Level _____ Day/Time _____

Name	Age	Stronger Foot

Strengths, Weaknesses & Notes

Student Info

Level _____   Day/Time _____

Name	Age	Stronger Foot

Strengths, Weaknesses & Notes

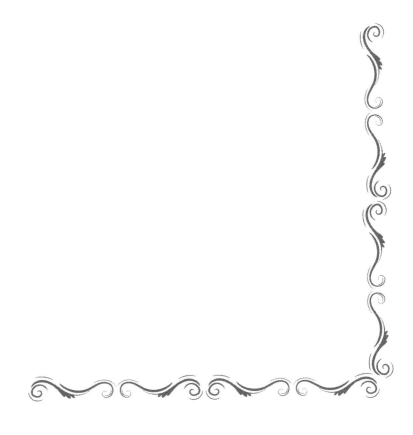

Student Info

Level _____ Day/Time _____

Name	Age	Stronger Foot

Strengths, Weaknesses & Notes

Student Info

Level _____ Day/Time _____

Name	Age	Stronger Foot

Strengths, Weaknesses & Notes

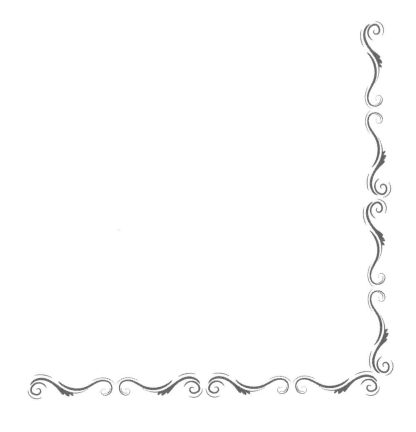

Student Info

Level _____ Day/Time _____

Name	Age	Stronger Foot

Strengths, Weaknesses & Notes

Student Info

Level _____   Day/Time _____

Name	Age	Stronger Foot

Strengths, Weaknesses & Notes

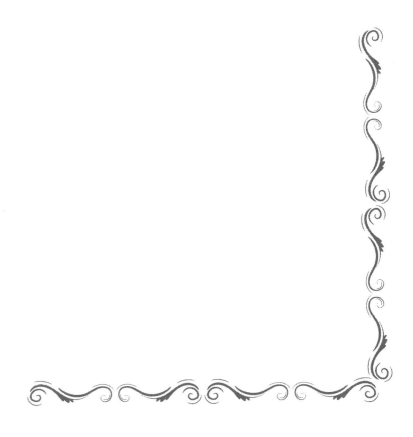

Student Info

Level _____   Day/Time _____

Name   Age   Stronger Foot

Strengths, Weaknesses & Notes

Student Info

Level _____   Day/Time _____

Name   Age   Stronger Foot

Strengths, Weaknesses & Notes

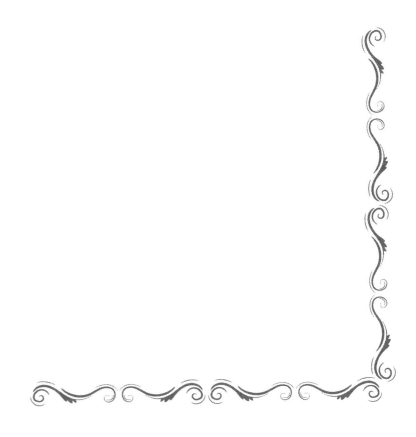

Student Info

Level _____ Day/Time _____

Name	Age	Stronger Foot

Strengths, Weaknesses & Notes

Student Info

Level _____   Day/Time _____

Name	Age	Stronger Foot

Strengths, Weaknesses & Notes

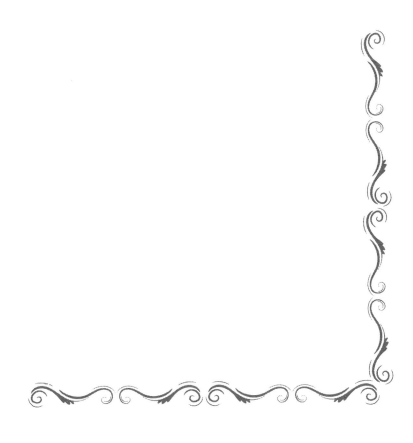

Student Info

Level _____ Day/Time _____

Name	Age	Stronger Foot

Strengths, Weaknesses & Notes

Student Info

Level _____ Day/Time _____

Name   Age   Stronger Foot

Strengths, Weaknesses & Notes

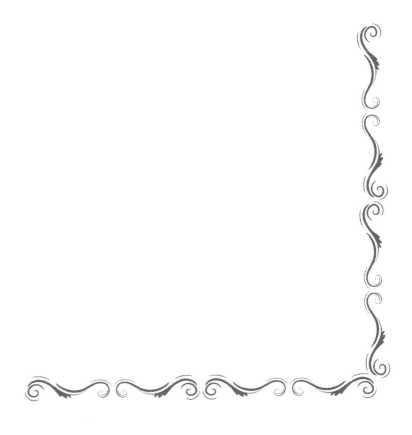

Student Info

Level _____ Day/Time _____

Name	Age	Stronger Foot

Strengths, Weaknesses & Notes

Student Info

Level _____ Day/Time _____

Name	Age	Stronger Foot

Strengths, Weaknesses & Notes

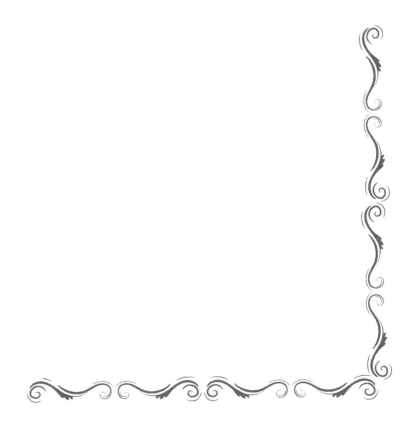

Student Info

Level _____ Day/Time _____

Name	Age	Stronger Foot

Strengths, Weaknesses & Notes

Student Info

Level _____ Day/Time _____

Name	Age	Stronger Foot

Strengths, Weaknesses & Notes

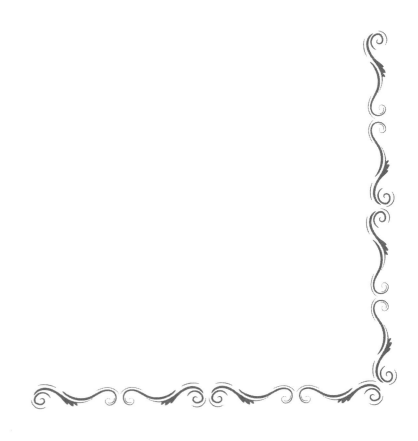

Student Info

Level _____ Day/Time _____

Name	Age	Stronger Foot

Strengths, Weaknesses & Notes

Student Info

Level _____ Day/Time _____

Name	Age	Stronger Foot

Strengths, Weaknesses & Notes

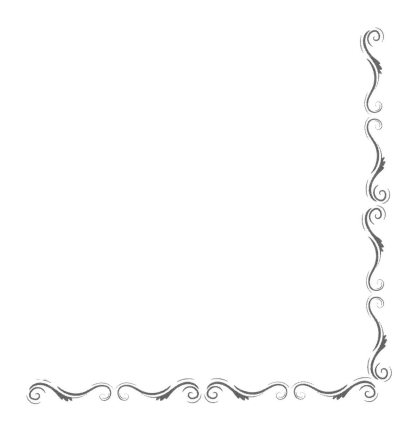

Student Info

Level _____ Day/Time _____

Name	Age	Stronger Foot

Strengths, Weaknesses & Notes

Student Info

Level _____   Day/Time _____

Name	Age	Stronger Foot

Strengths, Weaknesses & Notes

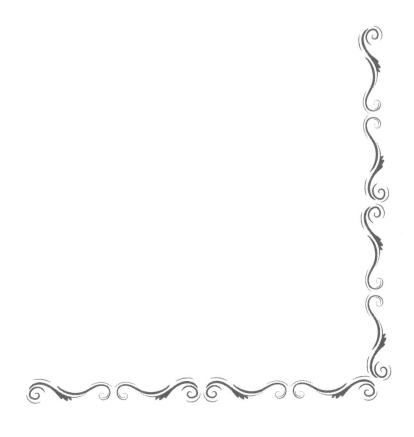

Student Info

Level _____   Day/Time _____

Name   Age   Stronger Foot

Strengths, Weaknesses & Notes

Student Info

Level _____ Day/Time _____

Name	Age	Stronger Foot

Strengths, Weaknesses & Notes

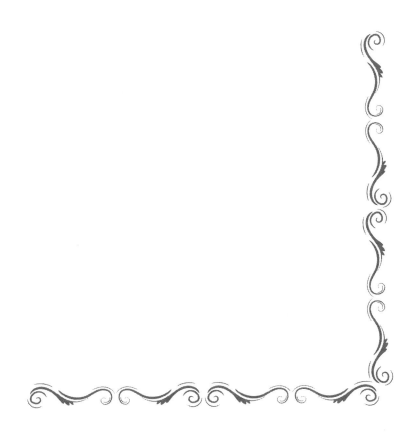

Student Info

Level _____ Day/Time _____

Name	Age	Stronger Foot

Strengths, Weaknesses & Notes

Student Info

Level _____   Day/Time _____

Name	Age	Stronger Foot

Strengths, Weaknesses & Notes

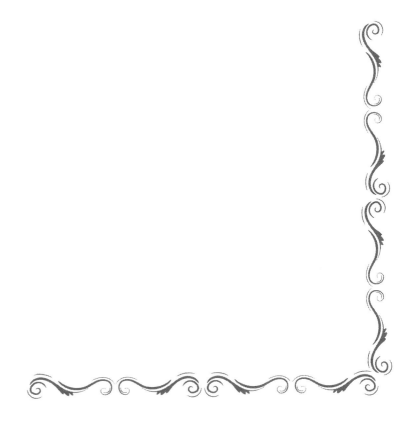

Student Info

Level _____   Day/Time _____

Name	Age	Stronger Foot

Strengths, Weaknesses & Notes

Student Info

Level _____   Day/Time _____

Name	Age	Stronger Foot

Strengths, Weaknesses & Notes

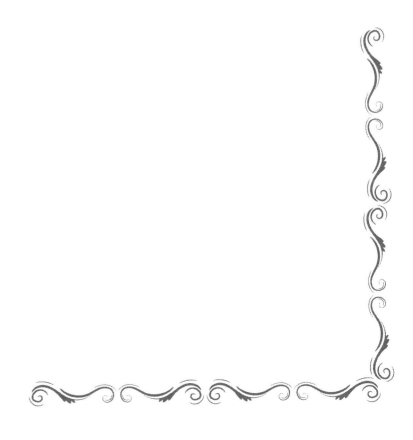

Student Info

Level _____ Day/Time _____

Name   Age   Stronger Foot

Strengths, Weaknesses & Notes

Student Info

Level _____ Day/Time _____

Name	Age	Stronger Foot

Strengths, Weaknesses & Notes

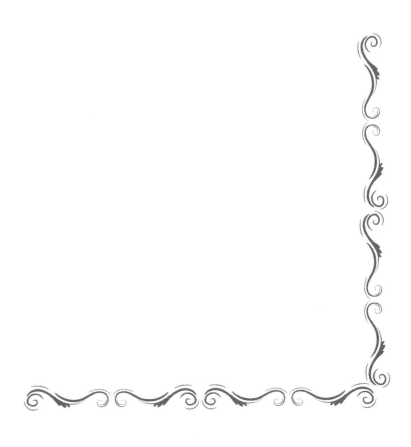

Student Info

Level _____ Day/Time _____

Name   Age   Stronger Foot

Strengths, Weaknesses & Notes

Student Info

Level _____ Day/Time _____

Name	Age	Stronger Foot

Strengths, Weaknesses & Notes

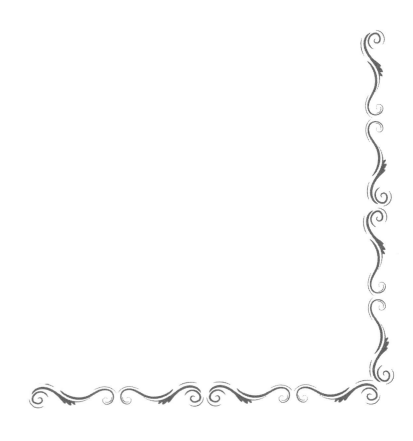

Student Info

Level _____ Day/Time _____

Name	Age	Stronger Foot

Strengths, Weaknesses & Notes

Student Info

Level _____ Day/Time _____

Name	Age	Stronger Foot

Strengths, Weaknesses & Notes

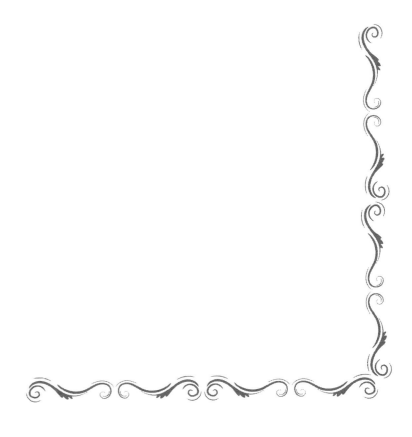

Student Info

Level _____ Day/Time _____

Name	Age	Stronger Foot

Strengths, Weaknesses & Notes

Student Info

Level _____ Day/Time _____

Name	Age	Stronger Foot

Strengths, Weaknesses & Notes

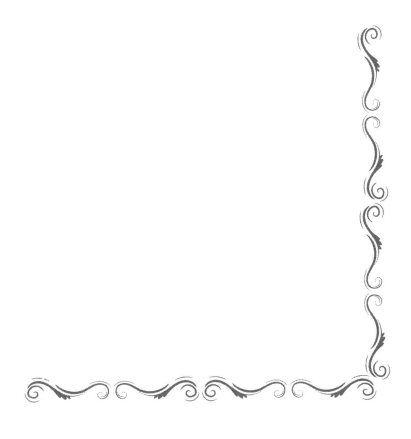

Student Info

Level _____   Day/Time _____

Name	Age	Stronger Foot

Strengths, Weaknesses & Notes

Student Info

Level _____ Day/Time _____

Name	Age	Stronger Foot

Strengths, Weaknesses & Notes

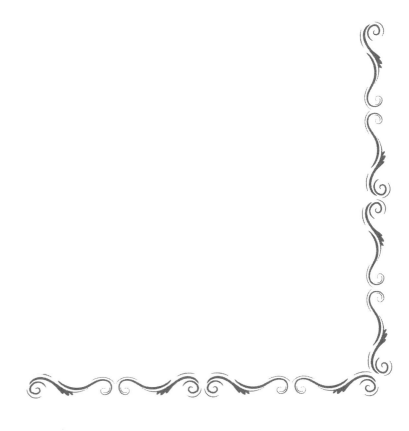

Student Info

Level _____ Day/Time _____

Name   Age   Stronger Foot

Strengths, Weaknesses & Notes

Student Info

Level _____   Day/Time _____

Name	Age	Stronger Foot

Strengths, Weaknesses & Notes

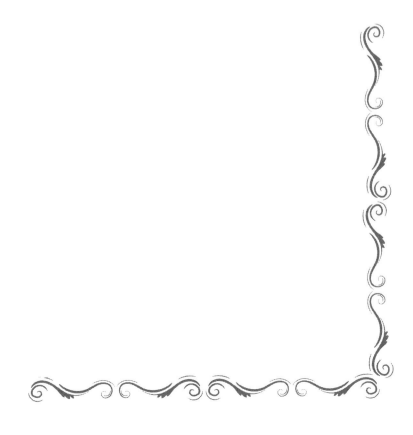

Student Info

Level _____ Day/Time _____

Name   Age   Stronger Foot

Strengths, Weaknesses & Notes

Student Info

Level _____ Day/Time _____

Name	Age	Stronger Foot

Strengths, Weaknesses & Notes

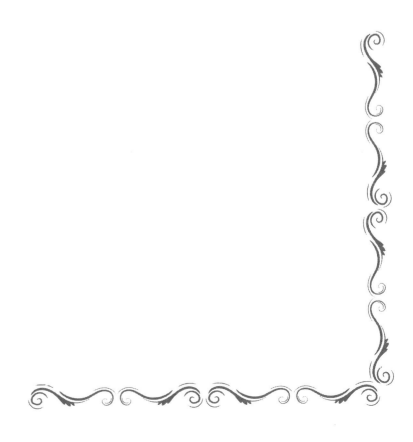

Student Info

Level _____ Day/Time _____

Name	Age	Stronger Foot

Strengths, Weaknesses & Notes

Made in the USA
Columbia, SC
09 August 2024